OXFORD

A MISCELLANY

Compiled by Julia Skinner
With particular reference to the work of Nick Channer

THE FRANCIS FRITH COLLECTION

www.francisfrith.com

Based on a book first published in the United Kingdom in 2006 by The Francis Frith Collection®

This edition published exclusively for Oakridge in 2009 ISBN 978-1-84589-431-3

British Library Cataloguing in Publication Data

Did You Know? Oxford - A Miscellany
Compiled by Julia Skinner
With particular reference to the work of Nick Channer

The Francis Frith Collection
Frith's Barn, Teffont,
Salisbury, Wiltshire SP3 5QP
Tel: +44 (0) 1722 716 376
Email: info@francisfrith.co.uk
www.francisfrith.com

Printed and bound in Singapore

Front Cover: **OXFORD, CORNMARKET STREET 1922** 71996p

The colour-tinting is for illustrative purposes only, and is not intended to be historically accurate

CONTENTS

2   Introduction

4   Oxfordshire Dialect Words and
    Phrases

5   Haunted Oxford

6   Oxford Miscellany

42 Sporting Oxford

44 Quiz Questions

46 Recipes

50 Quiz Answers

54 Francis Frith - Pioneer Victorian
    Photographer

INTRODUCTION

The beauty of Oxford has inspired several writers to heights of poetic description. Matthew Arnold called it 'that sweet city with her dreaming spires', and Thomas Hardy's 'Jude the Obscure' likened the city to 'the heavenly Jerusalem'. Oxford ranks in importance with Rome, Athens and Paris, and can boast a huge and varied assortment of ancient buildings, monuments and treasured landmarks, surrounded by the houses, shops and offices of a bustling modern city.

Oxford was originally an Anglo-Saxon town, and King Alfred the Great set up a mint there in AD879. By the mid 12th century Oxford was an important town with a royal palace, city walls, and numerous churches and monastic houses. The university which eventually produced that vision of dreaming spires and golden limestone began quite informally with groups of students gathering around priests. These teachers or doctors found royal and other noble patronage, and matters advanced during the 12th century, when the masters taught scholars who lived in halls. In the 13th century the college system began, with masters and scholars living in one complex of buildings; the earliest colleges were University, Balliol and Merton Colleges. 'Oxford University' is made up of a federation of about 40 colleges, each of which is virtually autonomous, with its own rules and administration. The real core of the university is formed by Oxford's world-famous landmarks, such as the Radcliffe Camera, the Sheldonian Theatre, the Divinity School and the Bodleian Library.

The university and its colleges built many buildings of outstanding architectural and historic interest, the whole ensemble

still quite breathtaking to a visitor. In recent years millions of pounds have been spent on the city, restoring and cleaning the stonework of the colleges and university buildings, which had become grimy and black with the passage of time. The utmost care was taken in preserving them; today this great seat of learning, designed by distinguished architects such as Christopher Wren and Nicholas Hawksmoor, looks as good as it did when they helped to create it.

Oxford's rivers are an intrinsic part of the city's beauty and character. The Oxford stretch of the Thames comes to life during Eights Week in May, one of the city's brightest and most colourful attractions. Rowing boats and punts are available for hire at Folly Bridge, and river cruises can be enjoyed.

During the 20th century Oxford, like many other towns and cities, witnessed sweeping changes. The age of the motorcar had arrived, and in 1913 William Morris produced his first motorised vehicle in a workshop at Cowley. By the late 1930s the car industry had made an enormous impact on Oxford, with new housing estates built to accommodate the thousands of people who worked at the plant. The car-making industry at Cowley has gone through several company mergers and name changes; the plant is currently owned by BMW, and the New MINI is produced there.

There have been many other changes to Oxford over the years, but the city still retains its grace and elegance. It remains a place of infinite beauty, whose story is full of fascinating characters and events of which this book can only provide a glimpse.

OXFORDSHIRE DIALECT
WORDS AND PHRASES

'Airywig' or **'arrywig'** - an earwig.

'Akkard' - contrary, perverse.

'Argufy' - to argue or dispute.

'Cheese-log' - a woodlouse.

'Clack' - talk, chatter.

'Devil's darning needle' - a dragonfly.

'Devilment' - mischief.

'Maggled' - flushed with heat.

'Mommered' - worried.

'Masterful' - domineering, liking his own way.

'Mighty' - extremely, very.

'Many-legs' - a centipede.

'Moon daisy' - the Ox-eye, or Michaelmas, Daisy.

'Mizzymozzy' - a state of confusion, as in **'My head's all of a mizzymozzy'**.

'Oncommon' - remarkable, unusual.

'Scrat' - scratch, **'scrattin'** - scratching.

'Seemingly' - apparently.

'Take on' - to complain, grieve, lament.

'Yaffel' - a woodpecker.

HAUNTED OXFORD

Magpie Lane is haunted by a grieving 'Brown Lady', believed to be the ghost of a young Puritan girl called Prudence who died of unrequited love.

The ghost of Archbishop Laud, who was beheaded on London's Tower Hill in 1645 as 'an enemy to Parliament', is said to haunt St John's College, where he once studied and where he was elected chancellor of the university in 1630. The headless spectre is supposed to kick its head around the library floor.

Mary Blandy was executed in the castle yard at Oxford in 1752 for the murder of her father by poison, and her ghost walks in the vicinity of Westgate. A local tradition says that a blackbird perched on the beam of the scaffold during her execution, and no blackbird has sung in the area of the castle since then.

The headless spectre of John Crocker haunts the site of his tomb in the chapel of Exeter College. He was a famous Elizabethan scholar, and his shade appears in a costume of gown, breeches and a yellow jacket.

Obadiah Walker, who was the master of University College during the reign of James II, is said to haunt the room he occupied over three centuries ago.

George Napier was a Jesuit priest who was executed at Oxford during the reign of Elizabeth I. He was hanged, drawn and quartered, and parts of his body were displayed around the city. Napier's decapitated ghost is said to roam Banbury Road in search of his head, the only part of his body that it has not been able to retrieve.

OXFORD MISCELLANY

Oxford was originally known as 'Oxnaforda', and was a settlement of some importance long before the university came into being. It began with the foundation of St Frideswide's nunnery in the 8th century. It is mentioned by name in the 'Anglo-Saxon Chronicle' of AD912, which records that King Edward the Elder (son and successor of Alfred the Great) had made it a fortified frontier position in his defence of Wessex when it was feared that the Danes might attack from the north. The settlement grew, and after the Norman Conquest of 1066, William I appointed his comrade in arms, Robert d'Oilly, to be Oxford's governor.

Tom Tower is one of Christ Church College's most treasured architectural features, as well as a famous landmark on the Oxford skyline (see photograph 26815, opposite). John Fell, Dean of Christ Church and Bishop of Oxford, engaged Christopher Wren to crown the main gateway with this splendid creation in 1682, transferring the medieval bell known as Old Tom from the cathedral to the college. Since 1893 most of the stonework has been refaced.

Brasenose College was founded in 1509 and takes its name from the shape of an ancient brass door-knocker. According to some sources, the original brazen nose was carried off by rebellious students to Brasenose Hall at Stamford in Leicestershire, a rival seat of learning, and it remained there until it was returned to Oxford in 1890.

CHRIST CHURCH, TOM TOWER
1890 26815

THE CASTLE 1912 64171

Robert d'Oilly, Oxford's Norman governor, built a castle at Oxford in 1071, five years after the Norman Conquest, but all that is now left is the Norman tower seen in photograph 64171, above. Within the castle precincts lie the 'motte' or mound of Robert's castle and a Norman crypt.

During the Civil War, Oxford was the Royalist headquarters as well as the seat of Charles I's parliament. Christ Church College became Charles I's home for 3 years and his wife, Henrietta Maria, kept court at Merton College close by. The first phase of the Civil War came to an end on 24 June 1646 when Oxford surrendered to the Parliamentarian Sir Thomas Fairfax after a siege. The Royalist garrison of 3,000 men, which included the king's nephews Prince Rupert and Prince Maurice, were allowed to march out of the city with full honours.

The Taylor Institute at St Giles was founded with a bequest from Sir Robert Taylor, an 18th-century architect, and is dedicated to the study of modern languages at the university. The front of the Taylorian is characterised by statues symbolising the languages of France, Italy, Germany and Spain.

During the Civil War, Royalist forces defended Magdalen Bridge by throwing rocks down from the top of the striking Perpendicular bell tower of Magdalen College on to the heads of the Parliamentarian troops below. On May Day morning, the college choristers and the dons assemble at the top of the tower to sing a Latin hymn.

MAGDALEN COLLEGE AND THE RIVER CHERWELL c1950 O33110

HIGH STREET 1900 45183

Rising above the High Street in this photograph are the tower and delicate spire of All Saints' Church, built in the 18th century to replace a Norman church which was destroyed when the spire collapsed on top of it in 1699. The spire, a distinctive feature of the Oxford skyline, was designed by Christopher Wren's pupil, Nicholas Hawskmoor. No longer in use as a church, All Saints' is now the library of Lincoln College.

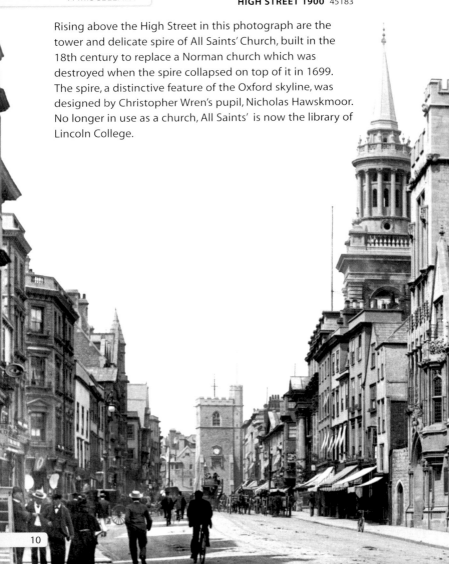

CHRIST CHURCH CATHEDRAL 1922 72009

Christ Church Cathedral, seen in photograph 72009, above, is not only the smallest of all English cathedrals, but also the chapel of Christ Church College, making it unique in the history of Oxford. St Frideswide's old nunnery church became the college chapel, and then in 1546 became Oxford's cathedral. The cathedral's official title is 'The Cathedral Church of Christ in Oxford'.

In 1870, when the Oxford dons still had to be celibate, the university opened examinations to women for the first time, despite great opposition. In 1873 Annie Rogers came top of the list in the local examinations, and she later became one of Oxford's first women tutors. Although all degree examinations were open to women by 1894, women were not admitted to full membership of the university, and thus able to actually acquire degrees, until 1920.

The famous Martyrs' Memorial in St Giles commemorates the 16th-century religious martyrs Latimer, Ridley and Cranmer, prominent Protestant churchmen who were burnt at the stake in nearby Broad Street by order of Queen Mary in 1555 and 1556; a plaque on the front of Balliol College marks the spot. The memorial dates back to 1841, and was designed by George Gilbert Scott. Hugh Latimer, one-time Bishop of Worcester, and Nicholas Ridley, Bishop of London, died together in 1555; Thomas Cranmer, the Archbishop of Canterbury, who was forced to watch his friends' execution, died a few months later in 1556.

THE MARTYRS' MEMORIAL 1922 72027

On the west side of St Giles is the famous Oxford pub, the Eagle and Child. During the Civil War it became a payhouse for the Royalist army. In the 20th century, J R R Tolkien (author of 'The Lord of the Rings') and C S Lewis (author of the Narnia books) met there every Tuesday morning between 1939 and 1962. Both were Oxford dons, as well as creators of notable fantasy worlds.

One of Oxford's most fascinating stories is 'the curse of Roland Jenks'. Jenks was a city bookbinder who in 1577 was convicted of being a papist; he was sentenced to be nailed by the ears in a pillory, and was so furious with his punishment that he laid a curse on the courtroom and the city of Oxford. The court proceedings became known as the Black Assizes, as it was believed that the curse had been effective when several hundred men in the city died within a few days. Among the victims were several court personnel, including two judges, a clerk, the coroner, the sheriff, and many members of the jury which had tried Jenks. At the time, the deaths were believed to be either a judgement by God on Protestants (the Catholic view) or a Popish plot (the Protestant explanation). Recent archaeological excavations in the area of the castle and Oxford's former prison have uncovered a mass grave of more than 60 skeletons which may have some connection with the deaths that followed Jenks's curse, although they are now believed to have been caused by an outbreak of typhus rather than divine intervention.

BALLIOL COLLEGE WITH TRINITY COLLEGE 1922 72020

Balliol, which claims to be the oldest of all the Oxford colleges, was endowed in 1265. The controversial Gothic buildings which overlook Broad Street were designed by Alfred Waterhouse and date from the 1860s (see photograph 72020, above). Trinity College, Balliol's neighbour, was founded in 1555.

Oxford's second university is Oxford Brookes, formerly Oxford Polytechnic, which gained university status in 1992. Oxford Brookes is famous for its successful history, modern languages, engineering, art and economics departments, and has been named 'Best New University' by 'The Times Good University Guide' for eight years in a row.

On the right of photograph 71992, below, is the splendid façade of Queen's College, a striking Classical-style building designed by Nicholas Hawksmoor. The first stone was laid in 1710, on Queen Anne's birthday. Beneath the cupola above the central gateway, though it is not clearly visible, is a statue of Queen Caroline, wife of George II, who donated £1,000 towards the completion of the quadrangle. Queen's College is named after Philippa of Hainault, wife of Edward III, whose chaplain originally founded the college to educate 'Poor Boys' from the north of England.

HIGH STREET 1922 71992

By the time that photograph 26948, below, was taken, Salter Brother steamboats were well-established on the River Thames, operating

Folly Bridge originally had a tower and gatehouse. This was known as Friar Bacon's study, and was used by Roger Bacon, the 13th-century astronomer and scientist, as an observatory.

Photograph 26946, opposite, shows one of Oxford's secret gems. The lesser-known St Peter's in the East is a fascinating old church which lies hidden beyond St Edmund Hall, and contains a vaulted Norman crypt beneath the chancel.

Major industrialisation came to Oxford in 1913 when William Morris produced the first Morris car at his new Morris Motors factory at Cowley. Car production had a great effect on Oxford, which now became an industrial city as well as a centre of learning. By the 1920s, the Oxford-built Morris Cowley car had overtaken the Ford Model T as the biggest-selling car in Britain. Morris Motors later merged with Austin to form the British Motor Company, which later became part of British Leyland. William Morris, the founder of Morris Motors, was made Viscount Nuffield in 1938; he founded Nuffield College and donated millions of pounds to medical research.

The Museum of the History of Science in Oxford holds a fascinating collection of exhibits, including early astronomical, mathematical and optical instruments. In the museum is H G Moseley's x-ray spectrometer, with which in 1914 he discovered the significance of atomic numbers, making a significant contribution to the development of modern physics. The museum also holds a number of Islamic and European astrolabes, and some fine sundials and orreries - wheel-worked machines that demonstrated the movements of the heavenly bodies.

The River Cherwell, also known in Oxford as the Isis, flows under the balustraded parapets of Magdalen Bridge in photograph 71999, opposite. Completed in 1782, the bridge has traditionally featured in May Week and other frolics as an impromptu diving platform.

One of the strangest landmarks in the world can be seen on the roof of 2 New High Street, Headington; the house is the home of Bill Heine, an American who came to Oxford to study and who is now a BBC Radio Oxford presenter. On the roof of his house is a giant fibreglass shark - 25ft long - which appears to be diving into the house. Heine installed the shark on 9 August 1986, the 41st anniversary of the dropping of an atomic bomb on the Japanese city of Nagasaki, and explained his reasons thus: 'The shark was to express someone feeling totally impotent and ripping a hole in their roof out of a sense of impotence and anger and desperation .... It is saying something about CND, nuclear power, Chernobyl and Nagasaki.' Despite several attempts by Oxford City Council to get the shark removed, it has now officially been allowed to stay.

'Oxford is on the whole more attractive than Cambridge to the ordinary visitor, and the traveller is therefore recommended to visit Cambridge first, or to omit it altogether if he cannot visit both.' (Karl Baedeker, from 'Baedeker's Great Britain', 1887, 30, 'From London to Oxford'.)

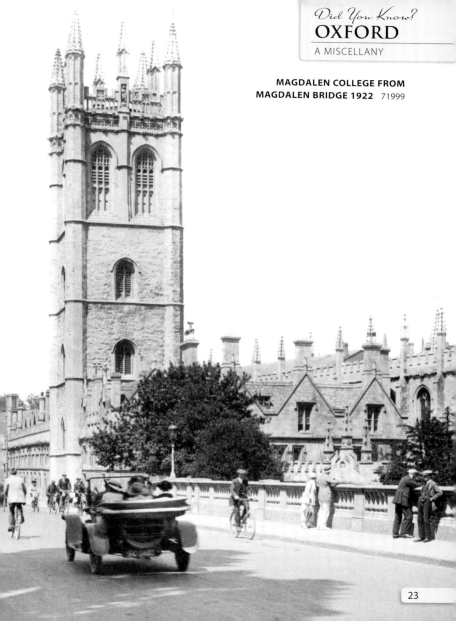

**MAGDALEN COLLEGE FROM
MAGDALEN BRIDGE 1922** 71999

CHRIST CHURCH COLLEGE 1890 26813

Christ Church College, the largest college in Oxford, was
founded as Cardinal College in 1525 by Cardinal Wolsey. Wolsey
dissolved 22 monasteries to raise funds for the project. When
he was disgraced it was refounded as King Henry VIII College.
Later it became known as Christ Church when the college
and the cathedral became one. Over the years Christ Church
has had many notable students, including three future prime
ministers: Robert Peel, William Gladstone and Lord Salisbury.
John Wesley, Lewis Carroll and W H Auden also studied here.

The area of Oxford called Jericho was originally the site of 'The Jericho House', which was used as an overnight refuge for people to stay in if they had reached Oxford after the city gates had been shut. The house was rebuilt in 1818 and is now a pub called the Jericho.

To the right of photograph 26942, below, is the Sheldonian Theatre, designed by Christopher Wren and opened in 1669. The theatre, named after Gilbert Sheldon, the 17th-century Archbishop of Canterbury, was built as an assembly hall for university occasions, and is still used for meetings and concerts.

BROAD STREET 1890 26942

The 11th-century Saxon tower of St Michael's Church is clearly seen on the right of Cornmarket Street in photograph 71996, below. John Wesley preached from the pulpit of this church in 1726. The tower is thought to be the oldest surviving building in

CORNMARKET STREET 1922 71996

Oxford; the chancel of the church is 13th-century. Until 1771 the North Gate of Oxford spanned the Cornmarket beside the church tower. This was also the site of the Bocardo prison, where the Oxford Martyrs were held (see page 13).

THE VIEW FROM CARFAX TOWER 1922 71986

CARFAX TOWER 1922 71997

Photograph 71986 shows the view from Carfax Tower, looking east down the High Street. In the foreground are the gables and turret of the Lloyds TSB building, designed by Salter and Davey and completed in 1901, but these are merely a prelude for the wonderful cluster of buildings beyond: Gibbs's Radcliffe Camera dome of the 1740s, Hawksmoor's twin towers of about 1720, and the two spires closer to the road. The nearer is All Saints' of 1710, and the one partially obscured is St Mary's, 13th- and 14th-century.

In a BBC radio commentary on the Oxford-Cambridge Boat Race in 1983, John Snagge famously remarked that the fog meant that he could not see who was in the lead, but it was either Oxford or Cambridge. He was unaware of making this gaffe until he heard a recording later!

Carfax stands at the crossing point where the original north to south and east to west routes ran through Oxford. Carfax probably derives from either the Latin 'quadrifurcus', meaning 'four-forked', or the French word 'carrefourgs', or 'crossways'. Carfax Tower is where Charles II was proclaimed king at the restoration of the monarchy in 1660, after the turmoil of the Civil War, the Commonwealth and Oliver Cromwell's Protectorate. Its clock is famous for its quarter-boys, which strike every fifteen minutes.

SOMERVILLE COLLEGE 1907 57393

Barely visible from the street, Somerville College was founded for women 28 years before photograph 57393 (above) was taken. It was named after Mary Somerville, a Scottish mathematician, and boasts two prime ministers among its graduates - the UK's Margaret Thatcher and Indira Gandhi of India.

One of the interesting items in the Ashmolean Museum is the lantern that Guy Fawkes was holding when he was caught in the cellars below the House of Lords in 1605, about to set fire to the gunpowder that would blow up Parliament and James I.

The church at the far end of the street in photograph O33130, below, is Wesley Memorial Church. Situated in New Inn Hall Street, it opened in October 1878. A new circular window at the front entrance, permitting views into the church, is etched with the words: 'O, that the world might taste and see the riches of his grace'.

ST MICHAEL'S STREET c1955 O33130

QUEEN STREET c1950 O33124

Until it was demolished at the end of the 19th century,
St Martin's Church stood at Carfax. The heavily restored
medieval tower, known as Carfax Tower, that is seen in
photograph O33124, above, is all that remains. St Martin's
was the city church, and a meeting point in times of war and
victory. There is a memorable view of Oxford from the top of
the tower.

Rollers

Dad would punt
us on the Cherwell
We had to walk
around Parson's
Pleasure.
We loved the
rollers !! :)

The Cherwell at the bottom of South Parks Road was blocked off to form what was known as Parson's Pleasure. This was used as a swimming pool which was popular with clergymen and academics, where the wearing of bathing costumes was not the custom. When boaters reached this blocked-off part of the Cherwell, any ladies on board had to disembark and the punts or other craft were taken through the swimming area by the men. At either end of this stretch of the Cherwell were rollers over which the punts had to be hauled to continue up or down the river - these can be seen in photograph 53705, below. The ladies had to take a path, out of sight of the nude bathers, to rejoin their male friends. If there were no males aboard the ladies had to wait until they could get help from men in following boats.

THE ROLLERS ON THE CHERWELL 1906 53705

THE EIGHTS 1906 53695

THE ALFRED JEWEL 1907 57416

The Thames is not sufficiently wide at Oxford for the conventional kind of rowing race in which one boat, known as an eight, overtakes another. The broad, sweeping movement of the oars requires a lot of space. Instead, the crews begin the race in line before trying to outmanoeuvre the one in front by bumping. The object of Eights Week in May is for each crew to move up one place in a complex table of positions maintained from year to year. Each year every boat starts off in the position it occupied from the previous year in the table. The position of head of the river and the second, third and fourth places are the most coveted.

Oxford's Ashmolean Museum is the oldest public museum in England. One of its most prized exhibits is the Alfred Jewel, shown in photograph 57416, opposite. This famous object was found in 1693 near the site of Athelney Abbey in Somerset. King Alfred retreated to the area around Athelney in AD878 to regroup his forces during his long struggle against the Danes, and after his victory at the Battle of Edington he founded a monastery in the area. The Jewel is made of gold and cloisonnée enamel. The figure on the Jewel has been interpreted as either a representation of Christ as the Wisdom of God, or possibly a personification of Sight. The function of the Jewel is unknown, but it may have been a book 'pointer' to help follow the text whilst reading, or alternatively it may have been a symbol of office, possibly sent by Alfred to one of his bishops or officials; there is also the possibility that it may have belonged to King Alfred himself. The inscription on the jewel in Anglo-Saxon, 'Aelfred mec heht gewyrcan', means 'Alfred ordered me to be made'.

OXFORD, HIGH STREET 1900 45181

The Oxford Canal, which was fully opened in 1790, linked Oxford with the Midlands; it joined the Grand Union Canal at Braunston and Napton-on-the-Hill, and linked Oxford with Coventry via Banbury and Rugby. For a while it was an extremely busy commercial waterway, particularly for the transportation of coal, stone and agricultural produce. The Oxford Canal lost out when the Grand Union Canal was completed in 1805, which offered a faster, more direct route between London and the Midlands. The Oxford Canal is now used for leisure purposes, and is widely considered to be one of the most scenic canals in Britain.

Founded in 1437 by Henry Chichele to commemorate Henry V
and those who fell at the Battle of Agincourt, All Souls' College is
distinguished by some of the finest architecture in Oxford. The tower
displaying the college arms was designed by Nicholas Hawksmoor.
The Radcliffe Camera is one of the reading rooms for the Bodleian
Library, its dome an outstanding landmark on the city skyline. It was
designed by James Gibb and completed in 1749. It was paid for by
a bequest from John Radcliffe, and originally housed a collection of
books provided by him.

ALL SOULS' COLLEGE AND THE RADCLIFFE CAMERA 1890 26859

The scenic stretch of the Thames by Christ Church Meadow has long been a rowing reach. At one time the bank would have been lined with eye-catching college barges, such as those seen in photograph 72056, below, which were used as clubhouses and

COLLEGE BARGES 1922 72056

grandstands. Sadly, most of these have now gone or fallen into decay, although a few have been converted into modest houses or holiday accommodation.

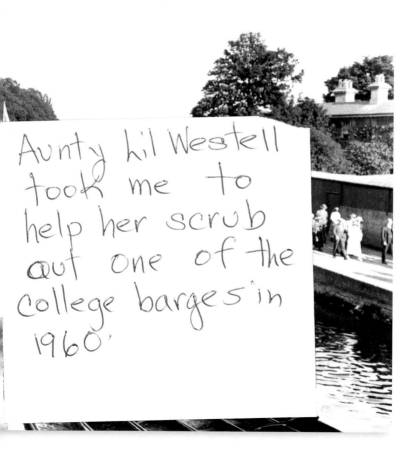

Aunty Lil Westell took me to help her scrub out one of the college barges in 1960.

KEBLE COLLEGE 1890 26853

HERTFORD COLLEGE BRIDGE 1922 72025

One of Oxford's most striking buildings is Keble College (see photograph 26853, opposite), characterised by its red and blackish-blue brick, polychrome patterns, bands, chequers, trellises and buff stone. Its exuberant design dazzles the eye. The college, designed by William Butterfield, was established in 1870 as a memorial to John Keble, where young men of limited means could be taught under the influence of the Church of England.

Another of Oxford's much-loved landmarks is the Hertford College Bridge, seen in photograph 72025, opposite. This outstanding structure connects the north and south quadrangles of Hertford College. It is sometimes referred to as Oxford's Bridge of Sighs in reference to the bridge of that name in Venice, but was not designed to resemble the Venetian bridge and in fact does not look much like it.

The oldest surviving book written completely in the English language is held in the Bodleian Library in Oxford. It is a copy of Pope Gregory's 'Pastoral Care', which is believed to have been translated from the original Latin text into Anglo-Saxon by King Alfred the Great himself. The Alfred Jewel in the Ashmolean Museum (see page 35) may have been one of the 'aestels', or book pointers, which we know that King Alfred sent to each bishopric in his realm with a copy of his translation of Pope Gregory's 'Pastoral Care'.

SPORTING OXFORD

Ever since the early days of speedway, the sport has had a strong foothold in Oxford. Speedway was introduced to the city in 1939 by the Oxford Motor Cycle Speedway Club. The club has enjoyed varying degrees of success. However, an undoubted high point was the 2001 season when the team won the Elite League. The championship was secured on 9 October, when the team drew at Ipswich.

Oxford United Football Club has had a relatively short, but very eventful, history. The club was formed after a name change by Headington United in 1960. Within two years the club had been elected to the Football League, and in 1985 was promoted to the First Division, the highest level of English football. This extraordinary achievement was eclipsed by the League Cup triumph of 1986. United won the prestigious national competition at Wembley, and put Oxford firmly on the football map. Sadly, the club then underwent a decline as notable as its rise, and in 2006 was relegated out of the Football League, ironically being replaced by Accrington Stanley, the club whose place it had taken in 1962.

The building of Oxford United's Kassam Stadium took over five years to complete. Work began in 1996, but was delayed for years by financial problems. The stadium hosted its first match in August 2001.

Martin Keown is one of the best-known footballers to be born in the city, in 1966. He started his career at Arsenal, and moved on to Everton and Aston Villa, before rejoining Arsenal. His career flourished on his return to Highbury, and he had the distinction of being a member of two 'double' winning teams, in 1998 and 2002. He played 43 times for England, including all 3 matches in the 1992 European championships.

Oxford-born Tim Henman is by far the most successful British tennis player of recent times. He has reached several 'Grand Slam' semi-finals, and was ranked number four in the world in 2002. Henman's career is all the more remarkable as he was diagnosed with a serious bone disease as a teenager.

Oxford was the scene of sporting history on 6 May 1954, when medical student Roger Bannister became the first man to run a mile in under four minutes at the Iffley Road track.

THE CHERWELL 1906 53704a

QUIZ QUESTIONS

Answers on page 50.

1. Who died horribly in Oxford after declaring 'We shall this day light such a candle in England as I trust by God's grace shall never be put out'?

2. What is a 'spoonerism', and what is the connection with Oxford?

3. The Oxford-Cambridge Boat Race is rowed over a course of what distance?

4. Which oddly-named parliamentary meeting took place in Oxford in 1258?

5. Oxford is twinned with five other university towns in the world - can you name them all?

6. The Bird and Baby is a nickname for which Oxford pub?

7. Oxford is the setting for the series of 13 Inspector Morse detective novels by Colin Dexter, which were turned into a long-running popular TV series starring John Thaw. What is Detective Chief Inspector Morse's Christian name?

8. By what name is Charles Lutwidge Dodgson (1832-1898), Fellow of Christ Church College, better known, and for which literary work is he most famous?

9. Oxford appears in Thomas Hardy's 'Jude the Obscure' disguised under which name?

10. The motto on Oxford's coat of arms is 'Fortis est veritas' - what does this mean?

LINCOLN COLLEGE 1927 79692

THE COLLEGE BARGES 1922 72051

RECIPE

ORANGE TART

Queen Street in Oxford is named after Queen Charlotte, wife of George III. This recipe comes from an old Oxford manuscript, and is believed to have been a favourite of Queen Charlotte.

Ingredients

225g/8oz shortcrust pastry
Finely grated rind of 3 oranges
400ml/14fl oz orange juice
Juice of 3 lemons
Finely grated rind of 3 lemons
150g/5oz caster sugar
3 tablespoonfuls cornflour
5 eggs, separated

Preheat the oven to 200 degrees C/400 degrees F/Gas Mark 6.

Roll out the pastry and use to line a flan tin. Bake blind, lined with paper held down by baking beans for 15 minutes, then remove the beans and paper and bake for a further 5 minutes.

Mix the orange and lemon rinds and orange juice with 100g/4oz sugar and the cornflour in a saucepan. Blend well and bring to the boil, stirring all the time. Lower the heat and cook for one minute. Remove from the heat and stir in the egg yolks and lemon juice. Pour the filling into the cooked pastry case.

Lower the oven temperature to 150 degrees C/300 degrees F/Gas Mark 2. Beat the egg whites with the remaining sugar until they form stiff peaks. Pile the meringue on top of the tart, to cover the filling completely. Return to the oven and bake for 30 minutes, until the meringue top is crisp and lightly browned.

OXFORD
A MISCELLANY

FROM MAGDALEN TOWER 1890 26802

HIGH STREET 1900 45182

MAGDALEN COLLEGE FROM THE RIVER 1922 72005

RECIPE

OXFORD SAUCE

Oxford Sauce can be used in the same way as Worcestershire Sauce. It is a piquant accompaniment to meat, especially cold venison, which was traditionally served at the high tables of Oxford colleges at College Feasts.

Ingredients

300ml/½ pint Port
4 tablespoonfuls redcurrant jelly
Juice of 1 orange
Juice of half a lemon
1 teaspoonful grated lemon rind
1 teaspoonful mustard
1 teaspoonful grated orange rind
1 teaspoonful finely chopped shallots
A little oil for cooking the shallots
Cayenne pepper to taste
Ground ginger to taste

Fry the chopped shallots gently in a little oil until soft. Combine the chopped, cooked shallots with all the other ingredients and mix in a liquidiser or blender. Store in a screw-top bottle.

QUIZ ANSWERS

1. Hugh Latimer, one-time Bishop of Worcester and a famous Protestant preacher. He was one of the Oxford Martyrs who were burnt at the stake in Broad Street in the 16th century.

2. A 'Spoonerism' is the term for the accidental transposing of the initial letters of words in a sentence, named after a popular Oxford character, Dr William Spooner, who was warden of New College from 1903 to 1924. Dr Spooner was famous for unintentionally confusing his sentences in this way. One of his most memorable mixed up speeches was the following admonishment to a lazy student: 'You have tasted two whole worms, you were found fighting a liar in the quad, you have hissed my mystery lectures, and you will leave at once by the town drain'.

3. 4½ miles.

4. The 'Mad Parliament' of Henry III at which parliament openly rebelled against the king, confirmed Magna Carta, and vested the government of England in a group of councillors led by the king's brother-in-law, Simon de Montfort. The king was forced to accept a new form of government, which was laid out in what became known as the Provisions of Oxford.

5. Oxford is twinned with: Bonn (Germany), Grenoble (France), León (Nicaragua), Leiden (Netherlands) and Perm (Russia).

6. The Eagle and Child in St Giles.

7. Detective Chief Inspector Morse's Christian name is Endeavour. Morse's first name remained a secret until the end of 'Death is Now My Neighbour', the 12th of the 13 books in the Morse series. The explanation for the unusual name is that Morse's father was both a member of the Society of Friends, or Quakers (who have a tradition of using 'virtue' names) and a fan of Captain James Cook, whose ship was the 'Endeavour'.

8. Lewis Carroll, the author of 'Alice's Adventures in Wonderland'. He first told the story to amuse Alice Liddell, the young daughter of the Dean of Christ Church, on a rowing trip in 1862.

9. Hardy called Oxford 'Christminster' in 'Jude the Obscure'.

10. 'Truth is strong'.

MAGDALEN COLLEGE 1890 26819

THE EIGHTS 1922 72063

52

FRANCIS FRITH

PIONEER VICTORIAN PHOTOGRAPHER

Francis Frith, founder of the world-famous photographic archive, was a complex and multi-talented man. A devout Quaker and a highly successful Victorian businessman, he was philosophical by nature and pioneering in outlook. By 1855 he had already established a wholesale grocery business in Liverpool, and sold it for the astonishing sum of £200,000, which is the equivalent today of over £15,000,000. Now in his thirties, and captivated by the new science of photography, Frith set out on a series of pioneering journeys up the Nile and to the Near East.

INTRIGUE AND EXPLORATION

He was the first photographer to venture beyond the sixth cataract of the Nile. Africa was still the mysterious 'Dark Continent', and Stanley and Livingstone's historic meeting was a decade into the future. The conditions for picture taking confound belief. He laboured for hours in his wicker dark-room in the sweltering heat of the desert, while the volatile chemicals fizzed dangerously in their trays. Back in London he exhibited his photographs and was 'rapturously cheered' by members of the Royal Society. His reputation as a photographer was made overnight.

VENTURE OF A LIFE-TIME

By the 1870s the railways had threaded their way across the country, and Bank Holidays and half-day Saturdays had been made obligatory by Act of Parliament. All of a sudden the working man and his family were able to enjoy days out, take holidays, and see a little more of the world.

With typical business acumen, Francis Frith foresaw that these new tourists would enjoy having souvenirs to commemorate their days out. For the next thirty years he travelled the country by train and by pony and trap, producing fine photographs of seaside resorts and beauty spots that were keenly bought by millions of Victorians. These prints were painstakingly pasted into family albums and pored over during the dark nights of winter, rekindling precious memories of summer excursions. Frith's studio was soon supplying retail shops all over the country, and by 1890 F Frith & Co had become the greatest specialist photographic publishing company in the world, with over 2,000 sales outlets, and pioneered the picture postcard.

FRANCIS FRITH'S LEGACY

Francis Frith had died in 1898 at his villa in Cannes, his great project still growing. By 1970 the archive he created contained over a third of a million pictures showing 7,000 British towns and villages.

Frith's legacy to us today is of immense significance and value, for the magnificent archive of evocative photographs he created provides a unique record of change in the cities, towns and villages throughout Britain over a century and more. Frith and his fellow studio photographers revisited locations many times down the years to update their views, compiling for us an enthralling and colourful pageant of British life and character.

We are fortunate that Frith was dedicated to recording the minutiae of everyday life. For it is this sheer wealth of visual data, the painstaking chronicle of changes in dress, transport, street layouts, buildings, housing and landscape that captivates us so much today, offering us a powerful link with the past and with the lives of our ancestors.

Computers have now made it possible for Frith's many thousands of images to be accessed almost instantly. The archive offers every one of us an opportunity to examine the places where we and our families have lived and worked down the years. Its images, depicting our shared past, are now bringing pleasure and enlightenment to millions around the world a century and more after his death.

For further information visit: www.francisfrith.com

INTERIOR DECORATION

Frith's photographs can be seen framed and as giant wall murals in thousands of pubs, restaurants, hotels, banks, retail stores and other public buildings throughout Britain. These provide interesting and attractive décor, generating strong local interest and acting as a powerful reminder of gentler days in our increasingly busy and frenetic world.

FRITH PRODUCTS

All Frith photographs are available as prints and posters in a variety of different sizes and styles. In the UK we also offer a range of other gift and stationery products illustrated with Frith photographs, although many of these are not available for delivery outside the UK – see our web site for more information on the products available for delivery in your country.

THE INTERNET

Over 100,000 photographs of Britain can be viewed and purchased on the Frith web site. The web site also includes memories and reminiscences contributed by our customers, who have personal knowledge of localities and of the people and properties depicted in Frith photographs. If you wish to learn more about a specific town or village you may find these reminiscences fascinating to browse. Why not add your own comments if you think they would be of interest to others? See **www.francisfrith.com**

PLEASE HELP US BRING FRITH'S PHOTOGRAPHS TO LIFE

Our authors do their best to recount the history of the places they write about. They give insights into how particular towns and villages developed, they describe the architecture of streets and buildings, and they discuss the lives of famous people who lived there. But however knowledgeable our authors are, the story they tell is necessarily incomplete.

Frith's photographs are so much more than plain historical documents. They are living proofs of the flow of human life down the generations. They show real people at real moments in history; and each of those people is the son or daughter of someone, the brother or sister, aunt or uncle, grandfather or grandmother of someone else. All of them lived, worked and played in the streets depicted in Frith's photographs.

We would be grateful if you would give us your insights into the places shown in our photographs: the streets and buildings, the shops, businesses and industries. Post your memories of life in those streets on the Frith website: what it was like growing up there, who ran the local shop and what shopping was like years ago; if your workplace is shown tell us about your working day and what the building is used for now. Read other visitors' memories and reconnect with your shared local history and heritage. With your help more and more Frith photographs can be brought to life, and vital memories preserved for posterity, and for the benefit of historians in the future.

Wherever possible, we will try to include some of your comments in future editions of our books. Moreover, if you spot errors in dates, titles or other facts, please let us know, because our archive records are not always completely accurate—they rely on 140 years of human endeavour and hand-compiled records. You can email us using the contact form on the website.

Thank you!

For further information, trade, or author enquiries
please contact us at the address below:

**The Francis Frith Collection, Frith's Barn, Teffont,
Salisbury, Wiltshire, England SP3 5QP.**
Tel: +44 (0)1722 716 376 Fax: +44 (0)1722 716 881
e-mail: sales@francisfrith.co.uk **www.francisfrith.com**